Beautiful You

Rachel King

Copyright © 2015 Rachel King

All rights reserved.

ISBN: 0986181986
ISBN-13: 9780986181986

DEDICATION

To every young lady who loves God and deserves a chance to show it through her life dream

CONTENTS

Acknowledgments	i
Unit One: Finding Your Identity in Christ	1
Unit Two: Having a Personal Relationship with Jesus	21
Unit Three: Faith and Relationships	39
Unit Four: Your Faith and Your Culture	59
Unit Five: Servant Leadership	77
Unit Six: Your Faith and Your Future	95

ACKNOWLEDGMENTS

Thanks to Marie and Lisa Holm who made the creation of this Beautiful You journal a family endeavor.

Introduction

Welcome to **Beautiful You**! You are a daughter of the King of the universe! Today, you begin a six-month Bible study designed to help you discover who you are in Christ, and how much He loves you. You are highly valued and favored by God, and He wants you to know just that. When you accepted Jesus Christ as your Savior, you entered into the Kingdom of God. In His Kingdom, God invites you to experience all the blessings, potential, power and promises He has to offer you.

Each month you will study a different theme, written especially for young ladies. We know there are specific challenges today for young Christian ladies, so we have designed a study that will get to the heart of many important issues. You will also have a mentor who will do this study with you. Each month consists of four weekly lessons that you will complete individually. After each weekly lesson, you and your mentor will discuss it together, as you learn from each other, and encourage each other along the way.

Ready to get started? Enjoy the beautiful Word of God as you study it through this Bible study. Let it feed you, teach you, challenge you, inspire you, and transform you, as it fills you with the joy and peace and hope of Jesus Christ our Lord.

Unit One
Finding Your Identity In Christ

True value and beauty come from being God's creation.

"Therefore, if anyone is in Christ, the new creation has come.
The old has gone, the new is here!"
2 Corinthians 5:17

Summary
This month you are going to be focusing on finding your true identity in Christ. Each week there will be a different topic that you will be focusing on. You will spend time praying and thinking over scripture to be able to understand how much God loves you, and what it means to be a child of God.

Weekly Topics
1. Being Who God Made You to Be
2. Your Value and Worth
3. The Love of Things
4. Put It into Practice

Week One
Be Who God Made You to Be

Study

This week you are going to focus on yourself. Be proud of who God made you to be. Who exactly did God make you to be? Do you believe that you are made in God's image and that He loves you just the way you are? This week you are going to take some time to meditate and understand this truth. Look up each scripture and fill in the missing words. Carefully read each scripture.

1. **Ephesians 2:10**
   For we are _____ created in Christ Jesus to do good works, which God prepared in advance for us to do.

2. **2 Corinthians 5:17**
   Therefore, if anyone is in Christ, the _____ has come- the old has gone, the new is here!

3. **Romans 8:37**
   No, in all these things we are _____ through him who loved us.

4. **1 John 3:1**
   See what great love the Father has lavished on us, that we should be called _____.

5. **Philippians 3:20**
   But our _____ is in heaven. And we eagerly await a Savior from there, the Lord Jesus Christ.

6. **1 John 4:4**
   You, dear children, are _____ and have overcome them, because the one who is in you is greater than the one who is in the world.

7. **Romans 8:1**
   Therefore, there is no _____ for those who are in Christ Jesus.

8. **John 15:15**
   I no longer call you servants, because a servant does not know his master's business. Instead, I have called you _____ for everything I learned from my Father I have made known to you.

9. **2 Corinthians 5:20**
   We are therefore _____, as though God were making his appeal through us. We implore you on Christ's behalf: Be reconciled to God.

10. **Romans 8:17**
    Now if we are children, then we are ____ – ____ of God and co- with Christ, if indeed we share in his sufferings in order that we may also share in his glory.

Meditate on these scriptures. Which ones stood out to you?

_____

_____

_____

_____

Meditate on Psalm 139:13-14 for a short amount of time before answering these questions.

> "For you formed my inward parts; you knitted me together in my mother's womb. I praise you, for I am fearfully and wonderfully made. Wonderful are your works; my soul knows it very well."
> Psalm 139:13-14

Here are some questions to help you think about who God made you to be.

What stands out the most in this verse?

_____
_____
_____
_____
_____
_____

What is the hardest to understand or believe?

_____
_____
_____
_____
_____

What are some of your God given gifts?

_____
_____
_____
_____
_____

God made you very specific, and He delights in who you are. What do you like to do for fun?

_____

_____

_____

_____

_____

How do you express yourself?

_____

_____

_____

_____

_____

When you have doubts about who you are, remember that God created you in HIS image. He loves you and is so proud of you. Continue to think about who you are as a child of God.

"So God created mankind in his image, in the image of God he created them; male and female he created them."
Genesis 1:27

What are some of your strengths? Weaknesses?

_____

_____

_____

_____

_____

God made you in a unique way, giving you specific gifts and dreams and talents. He desires that you use those to further His kingdom, and to live a full life glorifying Him. Have some fun thinking about those gifts He's given you, and how you might want to use them in your life.

If you could do anything in the world, what would you do?

_____
_____
_____
_____
_____
_____

What kind of job do you want?

_____
_____
_____
_____
_____
_____

What are you passionate about?

_____
_____
_____
_____
_____
_____

Prayer

God made you specifically just the way you are. It's tempting to give in to insecurities and doubts, but you are a child of God. John 1:12 says, "Yet to all who did receive Him, to those who believe in His name, He gave the right to become children of God." You have been given the greatest gift, the gift of being welcomed into God's family. Think and pray about what it means to have been created in God's image. Thank Him for the unique gifts and passions He has given you. Write out a prayer to God.

_____

_____

_____

_____

_____

_____

_____

_____

_____

Activity

This week, continue to think and pray about who God has made you to be, and how you might use those specific gifts to honor Him. Thank Him for making you the way you are, and for creating you in His image. Make a list of ten characteristics about yourself. Then using the Bible write down ten things God says about who you are. If possible, hang both of these list where you can see them regularly to remind you of who you are in Christ.

Week Two
Your Value and Worth

Study

It's important to have both confidence and humility. It's important to see yourself as a beautiful, daughter of the King. You are to be confident in who God chose you to be, who He made you to be. He is the artist and He is very PROUD of His masterpiece. Every young lady faces insecurities, but you must remember that your value comes from Him, and Him alone. This can be hard at times. Everyone has insecurities, and doubts, and lies fed to them from people and the devil, to take away from God's truth. It is an ongoing battle, but it is important to continually give it to Jesus so that He may help you conquer the doubts you may have, and to be reminded that your value is in Jesus.

Write down what kind of insecurities or worries you are carrying.

_____

_____

_____

_____

_____

God is rejoicing over you. Do you believe that? The Lord wants you to be glad in the fact that He loves you, and protects you. Your value is completely in Him. Do not put yourself down. Self-hatred will block you from believing God loves you. Instead, recognize that you need Him to make you whole, then gladly receive His love.

"The Lord your God is in your midst, a mighty one who will save; He will rejoice over you with gladness; He will quiet you by His love; He will exult over you with loud singing."
Zephaniah 3:17

What is your favorite part of this verse?

_____
_____
_____
_____

When or how do you most feel God singing over you, and rejoicing over you?

_____
_____
_____
_____
_____
_____
_____

Young ladies seek "popularity" to make them feel accepted and wanted, when in reality, that acceptance is never fully going to satisfy them. People, even those who love you, will at some point let you down. No one is perfect, which means that human love is not perfect. Only God can perfectly love you, because HE is perfect. You might look to young men to fulfill your desires and needs.

A young man can be a gift at the right time in your life, and God desires you to love and be loved, but ultimately your identity and value needs to be in Jesus first. This is not always easy, and you might feel alone. But you are not alone. That is why you must turn to Jesus to fulfill you so that no matter who hurts you, your trust is in the Lord.

> **"Am I now trying to win the approval of human beings, or of God? Or am I trying to please people? If I were still trying to please people, I would not be a servant of Christ."**
> Galatians 1:10

Meditate on that verse for a while. Do you think you seek people's approval? How?

_____

_____

_____

_____

_____

What is the hardest thing about seeking value in Christ's approval, and not man's?

_____

_____

_____

_____

_____

As important as it is to be confident in Jesus, it's important to recognize that we are fallen human beings often at fault. We need to have humility so that we can see when God wants to help us grow and change to be better images of Him; better lights to the world.

> **"When pride comes, then comes disgrace, but with the humble is wisdom."**
> Proverbs 11:2

In what areas of your life do you struggle with pride?

_____

_____

_____

_____

_____

> **"For all have sinned and fall short of the glory of God."**
> Romans 3:23

Is there anything you need to ask forgiveness for? Just like people are going to fall short loving you, we fall short loving and serving God.

_____

_____

_____

_____

_____

Prayer

Write down a prayer to thank God for loving you, singing over you, and saving you. Your value and worth lies completely in God, the creator of the universe, and that is incredibly remarkable. Don't take lightly the gift of love God has given you.

_____
_____
_____
_____
_____
_____
_____
_____
_____
_____
_____
_____

Activity

Show someone else, maybe someone you know who doesn't have many friends or is going through something difficult, that God is singing over them. Create a card or do something creative, or ask to pray for them. Go out of your comfort zone and challenge yourself.

Week Three
The Love of Things

Study

We all are tempted by material things. But God does not want you to put your love and value in that. It does not matter how much money you have or how successful you are in life, because those things will fade. What matters is what you do with what you are given. If you focus on earthly things, your heart will be consumed, even though it will never satisfy you. You will always want the next best thing, the next big event, something else to keep you motivated. Your heart must belong to Jesus first, so that whatever your earthly situation is you are content in Him.

> **"Do not store up for yourself treasures on earth, where moths and vermin destroy, and where thieves break in and steal. But store up for yourselves treasures in heaven, where moths and vermin do not destroy, and where thieves do not break in and steal. For where your treasure is, there your heart will be also."**
> Matthew 6:19-21

Do you find it tempting to put your value into earthly things? Explain.

_____
_____
_____
_____
_____
_____
_____

"Your beauty should not come from outward adornment, such as elaborate hairstyles and the wearing of gold jewelry or fine clothes. Rather it should be that of your inner self, the unfading beauty of a gentle and quiet spirit, which is of great worth in God's sight."
1 Peter 3:3-4

Do you think it is wrong to live comfortably? Or have nice things?

_____
_____
_____
_____
_____

What are ways you could honor God with the things you have?

_____
_____
_____
_____
_____

What of this world is tempting to you?

_____
_____
_____
_____
_____

What does it mean to store up our treasures in Heaven?

_____

_____

_____

_____

_____

_____

"If then you have been raised with Christ, seek the things that are above, where Christ is, seated at the right hand of God."
Colossians 3:1

How could you "seek the things that are above" on a daily basis?

_____

_____

_____

_____

_____

_____

_____

Focusing on materialistic things of this earth is a temptation. It is also a temptation to focus on our failures versus our successes. Do you find yourself comparing yourself to others? Or letting your "successes" determine if you're accomplished or not? Nobody wants to fail, but it happens. Just like others will fail you, you will fail yourself.

But there is hope! We can live our lives in the truth that our identity comes from God, who's perfect love casts out fears of not being good enough or failing in this life. The world tells you to accomplish much, have much, and be powerful. And yet, often times, that is not the story God has written for your life. You have to remember to turn to Jesus' plan to truly understand who you are. Your life is not determined by being the best, but by loving Jesus and following His calling. You will fail, because you are not perfect, but God is with you each step of the way guiding you through your successes and your failures. You cannot let the fear of failure stop you from trying new things, stepping out for Jesus, and taking risks for His kingdom.

> **"I have told you these things, so that in me you may have peace. In this world you will have trouble. But take heart! I have overcome the world."**
> John 16:33

What are you afraid of failing at?

_____
_____
_____
_____
_____
_____
_____

Do you compare yourself to other people? If so who?

_____

_____

_____

_____

_____

"So we have come to know and to believe the love that God has for us. God is love, and whoever abides in love abides in God, and God abides in him. By this is love perfected with us, so that we may have confidence for the day of judgment, because as he is so also are we in this world."
1 John 4:16-17

Do you believe that no matter what, Jesus loves you? Why do you believe this?

_____

_____

_____

_____

_____

_____

_____

Prayer

Take some time to think about what you are good at, and/or what have you been successful at? Maybe it is loving kids, maybe it is some of kind of trade, or speaking in front of people? Mediate on that, and ask God to help you use that to further His kingdom, and to take away any fear you may have of failing. Write down your prayer.

_____

_____

_____

_____

_____

_____

_____

_____

_____

_____

_____

Activity

Pray and think about something you really love, something you wouldn't want to just give away. Then think about why it matters to you, why is this "thing" special. Then give it away to someone, and see how living for God's kingdom is better than holding on to earthly treasures.

Week Four
Put It into Practice

You have studied many scriptures that tell you just how valuable you are. Look up the following scriptures. This is how God sees you:

You are a child of God – John 1:12

You are justified completely – Romans 5:1

You are free from condemnation – Romans 8:1

You have the mind of Christ – I Corinthians 2:16

You have been made righteous – 2 Corinthians 5:21

You have been blessed with every spiritual blessing – Ephesians 1:3

You are righteous and holy – Ephesians 4:24

You are redeemed and forgiven of all your sins – Colossians 1:14

You are a dwelling place for Christ: He lives in you – Colossians 1:27

You are complete in Christ – Colossians 2:10

You are chosen of God, holy and dearly loved – Colossians 3:12

You have been given a spirit of power, love and self discipline – 2 Timothy 1:7

You share in God's divine nature – 2 Peter 1:4

Look up each scripture and think about each one. Say them out loud. Pick 4 or 5 of your favorite ones and write each down on a small piece of paper. Tape them to your mirror at home, or in a place at home where you will see them often. Let these scriptures remind you of your true identity in Christ.

Unit Two
Having a Personal Relationship with Jesus

When we enter into a personal relationship with Jesus Christ, something wonderful happens: God begins to change our desires, and we want to be more like Him.

"Your word is a lamp to my feet, and a light to my path."
Psalm 119:105

Summary
This month is about your personal relationship with God. What exactly does that mean? Who exactly is God? The focus will be on spending quality time with your personal Savior, and understanding how important that is when living your life for Him.

Weekly Topics
1. Who is God?
2. Personal Quiet Time
3. Ways to Experience God
4. Put It into Practice

Week One
Who is God

Study

Read the love letter below from your Heavenly Father. Underline His characteristics (He knows everything, He loves, He can be found, etc.).

My Child,

You may not know me, but I know everything about you. (Psalm 139:1) I know when you sit down and when you rise up. (Psalm 139:2) I am familiar with all your ways. (Psalm 139:3) Even the very hairs on your head are numbered. (Matthew 10:29-31) For you were made in my image. (Genesis 1:27) In me you live and move and have your being. (Acts 17:28) For you are my offspring. (Acts 17:28) I knew you even before you were conceived. (Jeremiah 1:4-5) I chose you when I planned creation. (Ephesians 1:11-12) You were not a mistake, for all your days are written in my book. (Psalm 139:15-16) I determined the exact time of your birth and where you would live. (Acts 17:26) You are fearfully and wonderfully made. (Psalm 139:14) I knit you together in your mother's womb. (Psalm 139:13) And brought you forth on the day you were born. (Psalm 71:6) I have been misrepresented by those who don't know me. (John 8:41-44) I am not distant and angry, but am the complete expression of love. (1 John 4:16) And it is my desire to lavish my love on you. (1 John 3:1) Simply because you are my child and I am your Father. (1 John 3:1) I offer you more than your earthly father ever could. (Matthew 7:11) For I am the perfect father. (Matthew 5:48) Every good gift that you receive comes from my hand. (James 1:17) For I am your provider and I meet all your needs. (Matthew 6:31-33) My plan for your future has always been filled with hope. (Jeremiah 29:11) Because I love you with an everlasting love. (Jeremiah 31:3) My thoughts toward you are countless as the sand on the seashore. (Psalm 139:17-18) And I rejoice over you with singing. (Zephaniah 3:17) I will never stop doing good to you. (Jeremiah 32:40) For you are my treasured possession. (Exodus 19:5) I desire to establish you with all my heart and all my soul. (Jeremiah 32:41) And I want to show you great and marvelous things. (Jeremiah 33:3) If you seek me with all your heart, you will find me. (Deuteronomy 4:29) Delight in me and I will give you the desires of your heart. (Psalm 37:4) For it is I who gave you those desires. (Philippians 2:13) I am able to do more for you than you could possibly imagine. (Ephesians 3:20) For I am your greatest encourager. (2 Thessalonians 2:16-17) I am also the Father who comforts you in all your troubles. (2 Corinthians 1:3-4) When you are brokenhearted, I am close to you. (Psalm 34:18) As a shepherd carries a lamb, I have carried you close to my heart. (Isaiah 40:11) One day I will wipe away every tear from your eyes. (Revelation 21:3-4) And I'll take away all the pain you have suffered on this earth. (Revelation 21:3-4) I am your Father, and I love you even as I love my son, Jesus. (John 17:23) For in Jesus, my love for you is revealed. (John 17:26) He is the exact representation of my being. (Hebrews 1:3) He came to demonstrate that I am for you, not against you. (Romans 8:31) And to tell you that I am not counting your sins.(2 Corinthians 5:18-19) Jesus died so that you and I could be reconciled. (2 Corinthians 5:18-19) His death was the ultimate expression of my love for you. (1 John 4:10) I gave up everything I loved that I might gain your love. (Romans 8:31-32) If you receive the gift of my son Jesus, you receive me. (1 John 2:23) And nothing will ever separate you from my love again. (Romans 8:38-39) Come home and I'll throw the biggest party heaven has ever seen. (Luke 15:7) I have always been your Father, and will always be your Father. (Ephesians 3:14-15) My question is…Will you be my child? (John 1:12-13) I am waiting for you. (Luke 15:11-32)

Love, Your Dad
Almighty God

What stood out to you in the letter?

_____
_____
_____
_____
_____

Who is God to you?

_____
_____
_____
_____
_____

When reading the letter, was it surprising, overwhelming, or filled with truths you already knew? Did you feel loved and cared for when reading this?

_____
_____
_____
_____
_____

God is perfect. He cannot sin. There has always been and will always be one true God.

> **"For God so loved the world that he gave his one and only Son, that whoever believes in him shall not perish but have eternal life."**
> John 3:16

God is a perfect God. He has absolutely no faults, and yet He chose to save you by sending His own son to die. He wanted a relationship with YOU even though you're probably struggling daily with faults. How does this make you feel? Have you ever thought about it that way?

_____
_____
_____
_____
_____

Prayer

Take some time to really think about who God is. Find at least 3 scriptures that represent characteristics of God. Meditate on them. Ask God to show you more of who He is. After all, as a Christ follower you are called to be more like Christ so you must learn who He is and His characteristics. Write a prayer to God and ask Him to help you know Him more.

_____
_____
_____
_____
_____

_____

_____

_____

_____

_____

Activity

Take some quiet time to pray and re-read the love letter from God. Then write a letter back to God. Be honest with Him. Remember, you are talking to your Father.

Week Two
Personal Quiet Time

Study

Spending quiet time with Jesus is important. Reading His Word, praying, and listening for God to speak to you are tools that help you grow closer to your Creator. It is important that you have these disciplines in your life if you truly want to live for Him.

Do you currently spend time with Jesus? Do you enjoy it? Be honest with yourself.

_____

_____

_____

_____

_____

"Jesus answered, "It is written: 'Man shall not live on bread alone, but on every word that comes from the mouth of God."
Matthew 4:4

Do you believe that reading the Word of God is important in order to live a life for Jesus? Why?

_____

_____

_____

_____

_____

What comes easy about spending quiet time with God? Reading the Word? Journaling? How do you feel most connected to God?

_____

_____

_____

_____

_____

Do you ever feel confused when reading in God's Word? Why?

_____

_____

_____

_____

The truth is we all feel frustrated now and then. Sometimes the Bible can be hard to understand, but God's Word is eternal truth, and it will never stop helping, convicting, and encouraging you. Even when you don't realize it.

"Heaven and earth will pass away, but my words will never pass away."
Matthew 24:35

Prayer

Even though there may be times that you do not understand, you must set your heart to have the discipline of being in God's Word each and every day. When you read the Bible, ask God to teach you from His Word. Christians often times want a Word from God, a divine intervention, but they ignore the clear directions that have been provided to them to use WHENEVER in God's Word. You have a guide book from your Savior. Open it and see what He wants to teach you, or how he might want to lead you. Write a prayer to God concerning these thoughts.

_____
_____
_____
_____
_____
_____
_____
_____
_____
_____
_____
_____
_____
_____
_____

Activity

This week and from now on, spend 15 minutes a day, reading God's Word. Read and meditate on the psalms or read an Old Testament story, or one of the Gospels. And then truly pray over it and ask God to reveal something to you that pertains to your life. See how your days and weeks are different when you spend time in God's Word daily. See how much more you will discover about God himself, from His Word.

Week Three
Ways to Experience God

Study

God is the same yesterday and today. However, people experience God differently. You may connect with God on a deeper level through prayer, or being in God's creation, while someone else may connect more deeply with God during worship or reading Scripture. Now, all four of these ways to connect with God are important. It is important to read the Word, pray, worship and notice His creation on a regular basis. But it is okay to feel like you connect with your Savior more strongly in one way over another. Lets look at each one.

1. One way to connect with God is to be still in His creation.

> **"The God who made the world and everything in it is the Lord of heaven and earth and does not live in temples build by human hands."**
> Acts 17:24

Have you ever just gone out into nature and observed? Taken in the sights? The smells? Did you enjoy it? Why?

_____

_____

_____

_____

_____

"For since the creation of the world, God's invisible qualities his eternal power and divine nature—have been clearly seen, being understood from what has been made, so that people are without excuse."
Romans 1:20

Why do you think some people (maybe even you) really experience God when in nature?

_____

_____

_____

_____

_____

What does nature tell you about the character of God?

_____

_____

_____

_____

_____

2. A second way to experience God is through reading His Word.

But he answered, "It is written, "Man shall not live by bread alone, but by every word that comes from the mouth of God."
Matthew 4:4

It is crucial that you are in God's Word daily. It's a manual for life. What did you learn about reading the Bible from last week?

_____
_____
_____
_____
_____
_____

> **"For the word of God is living and active, sharper than any two-edged sword, piercing to the division of soul and of joints and marrow, and discerning the thoughts and intentions of the heart."**
> Hebrews 4:12

What did you learn from God's Word recently while completing 15 minutes of Bible reading a day?

_____
_____
_____
_____
_____
_____

> **"With my whole heart I seek you; let me not wander from your commandments! I have stored up your word in my heart, that I might not sin against you."**
> Psalm 119:10-11

Is this verse a prayer of your heart? Why or why not?

_____

_____

_____

_____

_____

3. A third way to connect to Jesus is through worship. As a Christ-follower you are called to glorify and worship God in all that you do. But sometimes, musical worship, through instruments, singing, and dancing help someone connect to Jesus on a special level.

Can you think of a time when you were worshipping with a song or a dance and felt closer to God? Why do you think that was? Was it the sounds? The visuals of dance? Or the words of a song?

_____

_____

_____

_____

_____

Do you play an instrument or sing? If so, do you feel closer to God when using those gifts? Why do you think that is?

_____

_____

_____

_____

4. A fourth way to connect with God is through prayer. Prayer is a powerful way to connect with God. Read the following scriptures.

> **"After he had dismissed them, he went up on a mountainside by himself to pray."**
> Matthew 13:23

> **"Very early in the morning, while it was still dark, Jesus got up, left the house and went off to a solitary place, where he prayed."**
> Mark 1:35

Jesus is our example when it comes to prayer. He prayed often. When we pray, we talk to God, and then if we are still in prayer, He often speaks to us in our spirit.

In Matthew 6:9-13, Jesus said:

This then is how you should pray:

"Our Father in heaven, hallowed be your name." – We are to worship God in prayer and thank Him.

"Your kingdom come, your will be done, on earth as it is in heaven." – Pray for God's kingdom to come, for God's will to be done.

"Give us today our daily bread." – Pray for all your physical needs.

"Forgive us our debts, as we forgive our debtors." – Pray for your spiritual needs.

"And lead us not into temptation, but deliver us form the evil one." – Pray for God's guidance and protection.

Prayer

Write a prayer below that either:
- Thanks and worships God
- Asks Him to meet a need of yours
- Asks Him to help you spiritually
- Asks Him to guide or protect you in a certain way
- Tells Him just what He means to you

_____
_____
_____
_____
_____
_____
_____
_____
_____
_____
_____
_____

These are four ways to spend time with God:
- A walk in nature
- Reading the word
- Singing a worship song
- Praying to God

Do you currently spend time with God all four ways? Why or why not?

_____
_____
_____
_____
_____

What is your favorite way to spend time with Jesus? Why do you think that?

_____
_____
_____
_____
_____

Activity

We discussed four ways to connect with God. Pick the one you do the least, and experience God that way this week. Then tell your mentor about your experience.

Week Four
Put It into Practice

Here are some different ways to experience God in a special way this week. Pick one and do it. Then discuss your experience with your mentor.

1. Go out in nature for a long time. Take a long walk, go sit in a secluded area for over an hour with nothing but your journal. Talk to God. Be honest with God.
2. Write a worship song. Maybe you love music and you really feel connected to God through worship. Have you ever written a song? If so write again, if not, try this new experience.
3. Read the book of John in one sitting. It'll probably take you a couple of hours, but take in the stories, and who Jesus is and what He says about our Father in Heaven.
4. Start a prayer journal. Write down particular prayer requests. Pray for them each week.

Unit Three
Faith and Relationships

"Be completely humble and gentle; be patient, bearing with one another in love. Make every effort to keep the unity of the Spirit through the bond of peace."
Ephesians 4:2-3

"A new command I give you: Love one another. As I have loved you, so you must love one another."
John 13:34

Summary
This month is about relationships. God has called you to be in fellowship with others. God created you to desire relationships, and to be surrounded by people who can challenge you and encourage you. Surrounding yourself with Godly people is important, and crucial to your spiritual growth.

Weekly Topics
5. Family
6. Friendships
7. Church Community
8. Put it into practice

Week One
Family

Study

We were not created to be alone.

> "The LORD God said, 'It is not good for the man to be alone. I will make a helper suitable for him.'"
> Genesis 2:18

Family is a central theme within the Bible. God created us to be in family, and we know this because once we are saved we are a part of God's family. His Word says,

> "For he chose us in him before the creation of the world to be holy and blameless in his sight in love."
> Ephesians 1:4

> "So in Christ Jesus you are all children of God through faith,"
> Galatians 3:26

He also created parents and siblings to surround us with encouragement, protection and support. He desires us to have a good relationship with them and to continue to build into the family unit.

> "Children, obey your parents in the Lord, for this is right. 'Honor your father and mother'—which is the first commandment with a promise— "so that it may go well with you and that you may enjoy long life on the earth." Fathers, do not exasperate your children; instead, bring them up in the training and instruction of the Lord."
> Ephesians 6:1-4

Describe your family unit. Are you close with them? Are you close with your extended family as well? Why or why not?

_____
_____
_____
_____
_____

Are strong family ties encouraged and celebrated in your community? In what way?

_____
_____
_____
_____
_____

In what ways are you grateful for your family? What specific characteristics do you love about them?

_____
_____
_____
_____
_____

What aspects of your family dynamic do you <u>not</u> love? What characteristics of your family unit make it hard for you to appreciate them?

_____

_____

_____

_____

_____

The people in your family are often the people you are closest to. Those you turn to in times of crisis, and in times of celebration. Family may look different to everyone. It may mean mom, dad, uncle, close friend, etc. Family are those people who are there for you no matter what. Even though you will have struggles, disagreements, and pain within your family, you know they will ultimately never leave you. But that can be hard if your family does not share your same beliefs.

Are your family members Christian? Explain.

_____

_____

_____

_____

_____

_____

_____

Prayer

If they are, take time to thank God for saving them and pray for their faith. Pray that their hearts will grow deeper in love with Jesus. If they are not, pray that God saves them and that they meet Him and accept Him as their personal savior.

_____

_____

_____

_____

_____

_____

_____

_____

_____

_____

Activity

Write a short letter of thanks to the family members you are closest to. Tell them why they are so important to you. (Remember, it can be your physical family members or maybe a spiritual family member.) Give them the letter – and a hug!

Week Two
Friendships

Study

> **"Above all, love each other deeply, because love covers over a multitude of sins."**
> 1 Peter 4:8

> **"Therefore encourage one another and build each other up, just as in fact you are doing."**
> 1 Thessalonians 5:11

In your opinion, what makes a good friend? What kind of qualities do they have?

_____
_____
_____
_____
_____

Do you think you have these qualities?

_____
_____
_____
_____

In what areas could you work on this?

_____
_____
_____
_____
_____

Who are some of your closest friends?

_____
_____
_____
_____
_____

Think about where you met them, and what it was about them that made you want to be their friend? And also, why are they still your friends?

_____
_____
_____
_____
_____

As wonderful as friendships are, they often come with difficulties and hurt feelings. Nobody is perfect, which means when two people interact and form a relationship there may be disagreements and heartache.

"Get rid of all bitterness, rage and anger, brawling and slander, along with every form of malice."
Ephesians 4:31

"Do not judge, and you will not be judged. Do not condemn, and you will not be condemned. Forgive, and you will be forgiven."
Luke 6:37

There are many more verses in the Bible that teach us how to treat a friend, and how to forgive a friend when they hurt you, which will happen at some point in your life. Friendships cannot grow with bitterness, jealousy or anger. That will hurt the friendship and eventually destroy it. Friendships need to be cared for continually.

Do you have anyone that you need to forgive? Why?

_____
_____
_____
_____
_____

Why do you think you hold on to bitterness and anger toward someone? What are ways to overcome your anger or bitterness toward friends?

_____
_____
_____
_____
_____

Is there anyone you need to ask forgiveness <u>from</u>? Have you hurt someone? Friendship can be challenging and at some point we all hurt other people. God calls us to be kind, and when we are not, we must repent, and ask the other person to forgive us.

_____
_____
_____
_____
_____
_____

Friendships are very important. You were created to have relationships with people. You might be someone who loves people, and for you this is very easy to understand and grasp. You love to talk to everyone, and you easily open up to people. Or you might be someone who thinks it's easier to do life alone, to keep everything inside and pretend you are always okay.

Which describes your personality more?

_____
_____
_____
_____
_____
_____

Why is it sometimes easier to run from people who care about us, rather than being open with them?

_____

_____

_____

_____

"My command is this: Love each other as I have loved you. Greater love has no one than this: to lay down one's life for one's friends. You are my friends if you do what I command. I no longer call you servants, because a servant does not know his master's business. Instead, I have called you friends, for everything that I learned from my Father I have made known to you."
John 15:12-15

As previously said, having friends is very important, but it is also important not to JUST have friends, but to surround yourself with GREAT friends. It doesn't do you much good to surround yourself with people who are going to hurt you or influence you to make poor decisions.

"Walk with the wise and become wise, for a companion of fools suffers harm."
Proverbs 13:20

"As iron sharpens iron, so one person sharpens another."
Proverbs 27:17

God's Word makes it clear that your friends should be uplifting people, people who are going to stand next to you through good and bad, and continually point you to Jesus.

Do your friends point you to Jesus, or direct you toward the things of the world?

_____

_____

_____

_____

The Bible also says to be a light to the world. So you might be asking, "How am I supposed to be a light to non-Christians if I am supposed to surround myself with Christians?"

> **"Therefore, as we have opportunity, let us do good to all people, especially to those who belong to the family of believers."**
> Galatians 6:10

> **"I have not come to call the righteous, but sinners to repentance."**
> Luke 5:32

You must live your life with balance. It is important to surround yourself with people who are uplifting, but it is also important to continue to reach those who do not know Jesus. We are not called to isolate ourselves in a Christian bubble. Jesus did not come to isolate Himself and relate only to the disciples, but reached thousands. And yet at the same time, He kept the disciples close to him. Together they supported and comforted each other in all that they shared.

Do you have friends who are not Christians? Who are they?

In what ways can you reach out more to non-believers?

Prayer

Write a prayer to thank God for the friends that He has placed in your life, and ask Him to challenge you in your relationships. Meditate on how you can be a better friend, and who you may need to reach out to a little more.

Activity

Think of someone that you need to ask forgiveness from. It could be a family member or a close friend. Go up to that person and apologize and ask for their forgiveness.

Week Three
Church Community

Study

Take some time and read 1 Corinthians 12:12-26. This is a passage that demonstrates how God has organized His church to be like a body.

What are your initial thoughts about this scripture?

_____
_____
_____
_____

Do you have a church community? If so, what is it like? If not, why not?

_____
_____
_____
_____

What role do you play in the church? If you are not involved in a church, why not?

_____
_____
_____
_____

> "For by the grace given me I say to every one of you: Do not think of yourself more highly than you ought, but rather think of yourself with sober judgment, in accordance with the faith God has distributed to each of you. For just as each of us has one body with many members, and these members do not all have the same function, so in Christ we, though many, form one body, and each member belongs to all the others. We have different gifts, according to the grace given to each of us. If your gift is prophesying, then prophesy in accordance with your faith; if it is serving, then serve; if it is teaching, then teach;"
> Romans 12:3-7

Have you ever thought about your specific calling in the church? Have you ever thought about how God's community needs YOU? And that YOU need the church.

Think of a time where your church community really helped you through something. What was it like?

_____

_____

_____

_____

_____

_____

As you learned last week, it is important to surround yourself with people that are going to build you up, and most importantly point you towards Jesus.

"Two are better than one, because they have a good return for their labor: If either of them falls down, one can help the other up. But pity anyone who falls and has no one to help them up. Also, if two lie down together, they will keep warm. But how can one keep warm alone? Though one may be overpowered, two can defend themselves. A cord of three strands is not quickly broken."
Ephesians 4:9-12

Can you think of a time that you helped somebody in the church? Maybe you prayed for them, or served them in some way. Explain.

_____

_____

_____

_____

_____

How did this make you feel?

_____

_____

_____

_____

_____

"Therefore confess your sins to each other and pray for each other so that you may be healed. The prayer of a righteous person is powerful and effective."
James 5:16

Have you ever confessed your sins to someone? Not just to God, but another person? If so how did it feel? If not, why not?

_____
_____
_____
_____
_____

Prayer

Living in community with other believers does not mean that we simply say hi to them at church, but rather that we do life with them. Think about your church life. Do you have people you are close to from your church? If not take some time to pray about how to get more involved. Pray that God would provide opportunities for you to meet people that could become trustworthy friends.

_____
_____
_____
_____
_____
_____
_____
_____
_____
_____

Activity

Confess a sin to your mentor. Maybe it is something you are continually struggling with like lust or anger, or maybe it was a one time act. Talk it through with your mentor and pray about it with her. Journal about how this experience felt.

Week Four
Put it into Practice

You have learned in this unit, that God has created us to have relationships in order to grow as people and as members of the family of God. You are a family member, a friend, and a child of God in His spiritual family. This week spend some time with a family member, a good friend, and a member of your church.

Unit Four
Your Faith and Your Culture

> "Do not conform to the pattern of this world, but be transformed by the renewing of your mind. Then you will be able to test and approve what God's will is—his good, pleasing and perfect will."
> Romans 12:2

Summary

This month the focus is on what society and your culture is telling you, versus what Jesus is telling you. Being a young lady can be hard, especially in a culture that is teaching the opposite of what Jesus teaches. How do you balance that? Can you be a part of both your culture and God's family?

Weekly Topics
5. Modern Pop Culture
6. Traditions
7. Salt and Light
8. Put It into Practice

Week One
Modern Pop Culture

Study

Do this popularity activity. List ten things that society would consider "cool" or "acceptable", then in the other column write out ten things that Jesus says is "cool".

What society says is cool	What Jesus says is cool

Modern popular culture is something you can't avoid. As a young lady it is hard, almost impossible to escape it. You are pressured to fit in, and to be living up to "today's standards." As a Christian young lady it's especially hard. You are being told to act and think one way (according to culture) and then you are told to act and think like Jesus. Often those directly oppose each other.

You may feel the pressure from media, or maybe even those who are close to you, like your friends. Sometimes they are the ones putting the most pressure on you to act a certain way, to be "cool".

Where do you feel like the pressure to "be a certain way according to culture" is coming from in your life?

_____

_____

_____

_____

_____

Do you find yourself wanting to be cool and giving in to peer pressure? How does this make you feel? Excited? Nervous? Judged?

_____

_____

_____

_____

Modern popular culture is influencing you even when you do not realize it. Society is saying, "this is what you have to do to be cool, and if you don't you won't be accepted."

"When he noticed how the guests picked the places of honor at the table, he told them this parable: [8] "When someone invites you to a wedding feast, do not take the place of honor, for a person more distinguished than you may have been invited. [9] If so, the host who invited both of you will come and say to you, 'Give this person your seat.' Then, humiliated, you will have to take the least important place. [10] But when you are invited, take the lowest place, so that when your host comes, he will say to you, 'Friend, move up to a better place.' Then you will be honored in the presence of all the other guests. [11] For all those who exalt themselves will be humbled, and those who humble themselves will be exalted."
Luke 14:7-11

Verse 11 says, "For all those who exalt themselves will be humbled, and those who humble themselves will be exalted."

Does your modern popular culture tell you to be humble? Explain.

_____
_____
_____
_____

Do you find that it is hard sometimes to humble yourself first? Do you ever feel like you need to brag about yourself so people will like you? Explain.

_____
_____
_____
_____

How does this compare to what Jesus tells you to do?

_____

_____

_____

_____

_____

Which is easier? Which do you think is most rewarding in the long run?

_____

_____

_____

_____

_____

Modern popular culture is always encouraging you to be the best, to have the coolest and newest things. Sometimes, it also pushes people to say mean things, to judge each other based on unrealistic standards of living and looks, and to isolate those that do not fit in. However, Jesus has encouragement that sounds quite different.

Jesus loves you JUST the way that you are. He accepts you for who you are, and wants you EXACTLY in the state that you are in. Modern popular culture sets up these "unrealistic standards" and gives the message that only when you reach these standards are you acceptable.

Jesus' message is that He loves you, and will save you now.

"If you declare with your mouth, "Jesus is Lord," and believe in your heart that God raised him from the dead, you will be saved."
Romans 10:9

Jesus doesn't give a list of tasks or qualifications you must meet to be saved. He says simply declare with your mouth and believe in your heart. That is it. Isn't it amazing that the King of the universe, the ruler of the world wants to save you, and have a relationship with you? When you think about it that way, it makes society's "acceptance" seem trivial and insignificant doesn't it?

Prayer

You may feel like you need to be prideful or win people's approval but you don't need to. You already have the approval and love of the only one who matters... God. If you think about that it will be easier to face your peers, to face what modern popular culture is telling you to be. Take some time to pray and thank God for loving you, and ask Him to give you strength to follow His teachings and His Word, rather than that of modern popular culture. Write your prayer here.

_____

_____

_____

_____

_____

_____

_____

_____

Activity

Jesus said, "The last shall be first, and the first shall be last." Practice putting others first this week 10 different times. For example, let someone go ahead of you in line at the store. You could also let everyone else get their food before you or help someone carry a heavy package. Write down the 10 things you did and then talk about it with your mentor. How did it feel?

Week Two
Traditions

Study

Do you have any traditions that you or your family practices?

_____
_____
_____
_____
_____

What are some of your favorite cultural traditions?

_____
_____
_____
_____
_____

Are there any cultural traditions that you no longer participate in because of your faith in Jesus? What are they and why?

_____
_____
_____
_____
_____

Have you ever struggled with balancing your culture and its traditions and your faith in Jesus? Maybe they go hand in hand with God's Word, which is wonderful. However, maybe some of them contradict Jesus' teachings.

> **"For God so loved the world that he gave his one and only Son, that whoever believes in him shall not perish but have eternal life. For God did not send his Son into the world to condemn the world, but to save the world through him."**
> John 3:16

What are your thoughts on how your culture and your faith can go hand in hand?

_____
_____
_____
_____
_____

Do you have people in your life that try to make you choose between your cultural traditions and your faith in Jesus? Explain.

_____
_____
_____
_____
_____
_____

"For I am not ashamed of the gospel, because it is the power of God that brings salvation to everyone who believes: first to the Jew, then to the Gentile."
Romans 1:16

"There is neither Jew nor Greek, there is neither slave nor free, there is no male and female, for you are all one in Christ Jesus."
Galatians 3:28

God's family is made up of many different people, from many different cultures. There are different denominations, as well as different ways to worship God. Christians are in many countries all around the world. Our cultures are very different, but our God is the same.

Do you find it hard to worship with people that are very different than you? Why?

_____
_____
_____
_____
_____
_____
_____
_____
_____

Do you think God wants us to worship with those that are different from us? Why?

_____
_____
_____
_____
_____

Prayer

Take some time and meditate on your cultural traditions as well as your Christian traditions. They might be the same, or they might be very different. Write a prayer and thank God for the ability to worship in a way that fits your culture.

_____
_____
_____
_____
_____
_____
_____
_____
_____
_____

Activity

Research the way Christians live in a country very different from yours. How does their culture help them to worship freely, or hinder them in their freedom of faith? Share what you learned with your mentor.

Week Three
Salt and Light

Study

As talked about in the first week of this month, often times when you serve Jesus you are going against modern popular culture. One way that happens is when Christ followers reach out and love people who society believes are unimportant, unclean, or "uncool." Society often ignores people like that, and this goes against everything that God teaches. He wants His followers to love everyone!

His Word says,

> "Then the King will say to those on his right, 'Come, you who are blessed by my Father; take your inheritance, the kingdom prepared for you since the creation of the world. [35] For I was hungry and you gave me something to eat, I was thirsty and you gave me something to drink, I was a stranger and you invited me in, [36] I needed clothes and you clothed me, I was sick and you looked after me, I was in prison and you came to visit me.' [37] "Then the righteous will answer Him, 'Lord, when did we see you hungry and feed you, or thirsty and give you something to drink? [38] When did we see you a stranger and invite you in, or needing clothes and clothe you? [39] When did we see you sick or in prison and go to visit you?'
> [40] "The King will reply, 'Truly I tell you, whatever you did for one of the least of these brothers and sisters of mine, you did for me.'"
> Matthew 25:34-40

We are called to love those who nobody else loves. Jesus came to pursue those who needed Him, those who were not "cool" according to society but those who were pushed away by everyone else. In doing this, Jesus was often ridiculed, as well as questioned. There's no doubt that if you live the same lifestyle as Jesus, you will be judged at times, or made fun of. As hard as it may be, it is important to follow Jesus' teachings rather than those of modern popular culture.

This may look different for everyone, depending on what your life looks like. It may mean becoming friends with the girl who nobody likes because she is "uncool". Or it may mean going to minister to the sick and homeless whom society has classified as unwanted or low class.

Can you think of somebody that your society has classified as "uncool" or "low class"?

_____
_____
_____
_____
_____

Have you ever talked to them? Why or why not? What happened if you did?

_____
_____
_____
_____
_____

"You are the salt of the earth, but if salt has lost its taste, how shall its saltiness be restored? It is no longer good for anything except to be thrown out and trampled under people's feet. You are the light of the world. A city set on a hill cannot be hidden. Nor do people light a lamp and put it under a basket, but on a stand, and it gives light to all in the house. In the same way, let your light shine before others, so that they may see your good works and give glory to your Father who is in heaven."
Matthew 5:13-16

Prayer

As a Christ follower, you are called to be the salt and light of this world. You have been given the greatest gift there is, a relationship with Christ, and you must spread this joy and goodness to everyone. It is your job as a Christ follower to help those who feel isolated and unaccepted, unwanted and disregarded, know that they are cherished and loved by the one true God. Pray that God would give you boldness to be salt and light in your world. Write your prayer here.

_____

_____

_____

_____

_____

_____

_____

_____

_____

Activity

Go talk to or spend time with the people or person you wrote down in this section that society has disregarded as being unwanted or uncool.

Week Four
Put it into Practice

Here are two activities to do this week as you continuing thinking about your faith and your culture.

1. Fast for 24 hours from something that represents modern popular culture. Some examples are social media, TV, magazines, going shopping, and putting on make-up.

2. Go to a popular place in your community, maybe a mall or the market place. Walk around and pray quietly to yourself for the people you see. Pray that they would accept Jesus as their Savior.

Unit Five
Servant Leadership

"For even the Son of Man came not to be served but to serve,
and to give his life as a ransom for many."
Mark 10:45

Summary

This month the focus is on how you can be a leader with a servant's heart. Jesus led thousands of people. He was not arrogant, but He was confident in who His father was. He knew that He was leading ONLY with God's authority, but He was humble and gracious as He led.

Weekly Topics
9. People Matter
10. God's Authority
11. Humility
12. Put It into Practice

Week One
People Matter

Study

Fill in the blanks of scripture. As you do this, think about how these scriptures help you be the best leader you can be.

1. **1 Peter 5:2-3**
   Be shepherds of God's flock that is under your care, watching over them- not because you must, but because you are willing, as God wants you to be; not pursuing _____, but eager to serve; not lording it over those entrusted to you, but being examples to the flock.

2. **Acts 20:35**
   In everything I did, I showed you that by this kind of hard work we must help the weak, remembering the words the Lord Jesus himself said: 'It is more blessed to _____ than to _____.'

3. **Luke 22:26**
   But you are not to be like that. Instead, the greatest among you should be like the youngest, and the one who rules like the one who _____.

4. **Acts 20:28**
   Keep watch over yourselves and all the flock of which the Holy Spirit has made you overseers. Be _____ of the church of God, which he bought with his own blood.

5. **Hebrews 13:17**
   Have _____ in your leaders and submit to their authority, because they keep watch over you as those who must give an account. Do this so that their work will be a joy, not a burden, for that would be of no benefit to you.

6. **Proverbs 29:2**
   When the righteous thrive, the people rejoice; when the _____ _rule, the people groan.

7. **Galatians 6:9**
   Let us not become weary in doing _____, for at this proper time we will reap a harvest if we do not give up.

8. **John 13:12-15**
   When he had finished washing their feet, he put on his clothes and returned to his place. "Do you understand what I have done for you?" he asked them. "You call me 'Teacher' and 'Lord,' and rightly so, for that is what I am. Now that I, your Lord and Teacher, have washed your feet, you also should wash one another's feet. I have set you an example that you should ___ _____.

9. **Ephesians 4:29**
   Do not let any _____ talk come out of your mouths, but only what is helpful for building others up according to their needs, that it may benefit those who listen.

10. **1 John 4:8**
    Whoever does not love does not know God, because God is ____.

Would you call yourself a leader? Why or why not?

_____
_____
_____
_____
_____

Do people listen to you when you want to share ideas?

_____

_____

_____

_____

_____

Think of a situation in which you had to lead. Were you gracious to those you were leading or more "bossy"?

_____

_____

_____

_____

_____

Jesus is the greatest example for leadership. Besides leading people, He taught one of the most important tools for sharing the Gospel. People matter. Love one another.

> **"Love the Lord your God with all your heart and with all your soul and with all your mind and with all your strength. The second is this: 'Love your neighbor as yourself.' There is no commandment greater than these."**
> Mark 12:30-31

Next to loving God with all your heart, loving others is most important. That is a pretty big deal. Do you find it hard to love others? Explain.

_____

_____

_____

_____

_____

Loving others is not always easy, especially if you are in a leadership role, and especially if they are not following your leadership to begin with. However, because you have Christ, you have His strength to love others. Think of when Jesus washed the disciples' feet. Some of these men would turn their backs on Jesus, and yet Jesus humbled Himself and washed THEIR feet, when really they should have been washing His.

How might you continue to make people your priority, remembering that people matter?

_____

_____

_____

_____

_____

_____

_____

The key to putting others first when you are a leader is to remember that your goal is to help them become a better person over all. You want them to be successful, to achieve great things, and feel confident that they themselves can be a leader. Most importantly though, it is not about them achieving great earthly success, but becoming another strong and confident follower of Jesus. You may be a leader with girls younger than you and not even know it. They may look up to you and your faith and your desire to read God's Word everyday. Your way of daily living can be a way of leadership in itself.

> **"Be devoted to one another in love. Honor one another above yourselves."**
> Romans 12:10

Do you think the way you are living right now is setting a good example for others? Why or why not?

_____

_____

_____

_____

Are your actions encouraging and inspiring those around you to make good decisions, or are you encouraging others to gossip, hurt others and be selfish?

_____

_____

_____

_____

Sometimes putting others first is not the "popular" thing to do. It may seem uncomfortable to lead, always putting others first. Or you may be tempted to lead with a selfish mindset. Many want to be in leadership so that they can be the boss and be in charge because they want power. That is not the way God intended His people to show His love.

Can you think of a time when you wanted to lead a group of people just to be the boss or to get your own way? Describe that time here.

_____

_____

_____

_____

_____

"Let us not become conceited, provoking one another, envying each other."
Galatians 5:26

Prayer

What are ways to keep yourself accountable when you lead? Think of at least three and write them down below. Take some time to pray about this, asking God to mold your heart to be a leader who puts others first.

_____

_____

_____

_____

_____

_____

_____

_____

_____

_____

_____

_____

Activity

Go out of your way to lead your friends in doing something nice for someone else. Come up with an idea and then ask your friends to join you in doing this activity.

Week Two
God's Authority

Study

As a believer, God has given you the authority to spread His truth around the world. You are a leader no matter what journey God takes you on. But the good news is you do not have to do it alone. You are being sent out in **God's authority**.

How does it make you feel that you are being sent out in God authority and that you do not have to do this in your own strength?

_____

_____

_____

_____

_____

_____

> "Humble yourselves, therefore, under God's mighty hand, that he may lift you up in due time."
> 1 Peter 5:6

John the Baptist said this about Jesus:

> **"He must become greater; I must become less"**
> John 3:30

What does it mean, "He must become greater; I must become less"?

___

___

___

___

___

Jesus wants to use you to spread his Gospel. Think about it. He doesn't have to use you. God could do everything on His own if He wanted to. But He chose to save you, and to use you as a disciple to spread His kingdom.

In what ways is God using you right now?

___

___

___

___

___

How do you think God could use you to spread His love and grace?

___

___

___

___

___

"His divine power has given us everything we need for a godly life through our knowledge of him who called us by his own glory and goodness."
2 Peter 1:3

Prayer

Ask God to help you lead others humbly, putting Him first. Ask Him for His truth to be grounded in you, and convict you when you fall short. Take time to pray and ask for opportunities to lead others as Jesus led, humbly and in God's authority. Thank Him for using you in the world to spread the kingdom. Write your thoughts and prayer below.

_____
_____
_____
_____
_____
_____
_____
_____
_____
_____
_____
_____
_____
_____
_____
_____

Activity

Spend some time in prayer this week specifically asking God to open your eyes to opportunities to lead through His authority in your life. Be on the lookout for these and then discuss it with your mentor during your meeting.

Week Three
Humility

Study

Humility is spoken of often in the church, and among believers. However, it is a lot easier to talk about it then actually live it out, especially when you are in a leadership role.

> **"He guides the humble in what is right and teaches them his way."**
> Psalm 25:9

When do you find yourself most prideful, and forgetting you are called to be humble?

_____
_____
_____
_____
_____
_____

Describe what you think a humble leader looks like?

_____
_____
_____
_____
_____
_____

Jesus was the ultimate servant. Even though He was the Son of God, He came to earth and became a humble carpenter. He humbled Himself so low that He became your sin and died on a cross, in your place. Jesus is the ultimate example of a humble, servant leader.

> "Do nothing out of selfish ambition or vain conceit. Rather, in humility value others above yourselves, not looking to your own interests but each of you to the interests of the others. In your relationships with one another, have the same mindset as Christ Jesus: Who, being in very nature God, did not consider equality with God something to be used to his own advantage; rather, he made himself nothing by taking the very nature of a servant, being made in human likeness. And being found in appearance as a man, he humbled himself by becoming obedient to death— even death on a cross! Therefore God exalted him to the highest place and gave him the name that is above every name, that at the name of Jesus every knee should bow, in heaven and on earth and under the earth, and every tongue acknowledge that Jesus Christ is Lord, to the glory of God the Father."
> Philippians 2:3-11

Jesus was completely focused on God through His whole life before the cross. You are called to the same way of living. Serving others with a humble attitude can be difficult at times, but if you keep Christ first, He gives you the strength, overflowing grace and love to extend to others.

It's also good to have other people in your life that can keep you accountable, and keep you humble.

Who in your life can hold you accountable to remain humble?

_____
_____
_____

"For by the grace given me I say to every one of you: Do not think of yourself more highly than you ought, but rather think of yourself with sober judgment, in accordance with the faith God has distributed to each of you."
Romans 12:3

Prayer

Ask God to continue to make you humble, while giving you leadership opportunities to help further His Kingdom. Write down your prayer.

_____
_____
_____
_____
_____
_____
_____
_____
_____

Activity

In this lesson, you wrote down the name of someone who could hold you accountable to stay humble. Ask them now to actually do that.

Week Four
Put It into Practice

Pick one of the leading activities listed below and do it! You can also come up with one of your own. Discuss your experience with your mentor.

1. If you are currently not leading, take on a leadership role. Maybe start a girl's Bible study, or volunteer with people younger than you, to give you an opportunity to put what you are learning into action.
2. Lead your friends in an afternoon activity. Plan whatever you would like to do. Think about leading as a servant, maybe asking what they would like to do. Practice putting others first as you lead.
3. Lead your family in a serving project for an afternoon. Figure out what it will be, where it will be, and how to put it together.
4. Discuss with your mentor an idea of your own.

Unit Six
Your Faith and Your Future

"'"For I know the plans I have for you," declares the LORD, "plans to prosper you and not to harm you, plans to give you hope and a future."'"
Jeremiah 29:11

Summary
This month the focus is on your future and the plans God has for you. This month will encourage you to listen to God's voice, dream big, trust God, and act on those dreams.

Weekly Topics
13. Dreams – God's Dreams and Your Dreams
14. Possibilities
15. Trust in the Lord
16. Put It into Practice

Week One
Dreams – God's Dreams and Your Dreams

Study

Fill in the blanks of scripture. As you do this, be reminded that God has a plan for your life and He loves you.

1. **Proverbs 3:5-6**
   Trust in the LORD with all your _____ and lean not on your own understanding; in all your ways submit to him, and he will make your paths straight.

2. **Romans 8:28**
   And we know that in _____ things God works for the good of those who love him, who have been called according to his purpose.

3. **Proverbs 16:9**
   In their hearts humans plan their course, but the ____establishes their steps.

4. **Ephesians 3:20**
   Now to him who is able to do immeasurably more than all we ask or imagine, according to his _____ that is at work within us.

5. **1 Corinthians 2:9**
   However, as it is written: "What no eye has seen, what no ear has heard, and what no human mind has conceived" the things God has _____ for those who love him.

6. **Psalm 37:23**
   The LORD makes firm the steps of the one who _____in him;

7. **Psalm 27:14**
   Wait for the Lord; be ____and take heart and wait for the Lord.

8. **Psalm 32:8**
   I will instruct you and _____ you in the way you should go; I will counsel you with my loving eye on you.

9. **John 15:7**
   If you _____ in me and my words remain in you, ask whatever you wish, and it will be done for you.

10. **Proverbs 16:3**
    _____ to the Lord whatever you do, and he will establish your plans.

"May the God of hope fill you with all joy and peace as you trust in him, so that you may overflow with hope by the power of the Holy Spirit."
Romans 15:13

Do you think about your future? Explain.

_____

_____

_____

_____

_____

What are some of your dreams that you have in regards to your future?

_____

_____

_____

_____

Do you believe that these dreams are possible? Why or why not?

___

"Trust in the Lord with all your heart, and do not lean on your own understanding. In all your ways acknowledge him, and he will make straight your paths."
Proverbs 3:5-6

"And we know that in all things God works for the good of those who love him, who have been called according to his purpose."
Romans 8:28

The key to thinking and dreaming about God's plan for you is to first think about what God cares deeply about, and then relate that to your passions. It is important to think about what God is passionate about first. What does He love?

What are some things God is passionate about?

___

> **"Never be lacking in zeal, but keep your spiritual fervor, serving the Lord."**
> Romans 12:11

Next, ask yourself a question. What are some of the world's problems? Pray and ask God to reveal to you what breaks His heart. What are issues that you as a Christ follower are called to help with?

_____

_____

_____

_____

_____

> **"Therefore, as God's chosen people, holy and dearly loved, clothe yourselves with compassion, kindness, humility, gentleness, and patience."**
> Colossians 3:12

Lastly, think about what you are passionate about. Or think about what you simply love doing. Think big. If you could do anything for a very long time, what would that be?

_____

_____

_____

_____

_____

Prayer

Take these three ideas: God's passions, the world's problems, and your passions. Now put them together and you may discover what God's best plan is for your life. With Christ, anything is possible. It's good and you should be encouraged to dream. Think about the circumstances and ways God could use you for His kingdom. He wants to use you! Do you believe that? Take some time to pray and ask God for the courage to do what He is calling you to, and to have an open mind to the possibilities of what is yet to come. Write a prayer.

_____

_____

_____

_____

_____

_____

_____

_____

_____

_____

_____

"I can do all things through him who gives me strength."
Philippians 4:13

Activity

Talk to at least three people (not including your mentor) that you trust, to encourage and challenge you, about your future. Talk openly with them about what you think are some possibilities, and ask them their opinions, and what they could see you doing in the future.

Week Two
Possibilities

Study

Have you ever dreamed about the future, but stopped yourself because you didn't think it was possible? As you get older, with even more uncertainties approaching, you must have faith in the Lord. There are times to be realistic about your life, but you must also remind yourself that God is a miracle working God.

> **"For the Spirit God gave us does not make us timid, but gives us power, love, and self-discipline."**
> 2 Timothy 1:7

God wants us to dream in big ways. It is okay to dream for yourself, but ultimately the way that God wants you to think is to be bold, and think big, for Him. You are called to live a life that glorifies Him, and that brings Him honor.

> **"As for God, his way is perfect: The Lord's word is flawless; he shields all who take refuge in him."**
> Psalm 18:30

Do you believe that you could do anything for God's kingdom? Why or why not?

_____

_____

_____

_____

_____

Have you ever felt called to a specific lifestyle or ministry? If so, what was it?

_____

_____

_____

_____

Have you ever dreamed about doing something for God's kingdom but then denied yourself the thoughts? Why?

_____

_____

_____

_____

> **"Commit your way to the Lord whatever you do, and he will establish your plans."**
> Psalm 16:3

Prayer

Remember this. You cannot simply dream about what you could do, and then expect God to miraculously put it into action. God wants you to act first. He needs you to take a leap of faith, to create something, to TRY something. It is very possible that the first thing, or even the first few things you try will fail. Be patient. Pray through it. And trust that God will lead you in the direction He wants you to go.

What is something you would want to try?

_____
_____
_____
_____
_____

What do you think is holding you back?

_____
_____
_____
_____
_____

Do you think your friends and family would encourage you to take a leap of faith, or be safe and cautious about your future?

_____
_____
_____
_____
_____

God has a plan for your life, and no matter what it is, He is working everything together for the good of those who love Him. Be patient in that.

> **"Wait for the Lord; be strong, and let your heart take courage; wait for the Lord."**
> Psalm 27:14

Activity

Think of three things you would like to try but they frighten you or you think they are impossible to accomplish. Write them down. Share those with your mentor when you meet with her.

_____

_____

_____

_____

_____

_____

_____

_____

_____

_____

_____

_____

Week Three
Trusting in God

Study

There are many, many scriptures that tells you not to worry about your future. It is a common theme and repeated idea that you should not stress about your future, or anything else for that matter. Easier said than done, right?

Do you worry easily? When? About what?

_____

_____

_____

_____

_____

> "Rejoice in the Lord always. I will say it again: Rejoice! Let your gentleness be evident to all. The Lord is near. Do not be anxious about anything but in every situation by prayer and petition, with thanksgiving, present your requests to God."
> Philippians 4:4-6

What does this verse tell us to do INSTEAD of worrying?

_____

_____

_____

_____

_____

What do you think your life would be like if you thanked God and then prayed about a situation instead of worrying about it?

_____

_____

_____

_____

_____

A lot of times, worry comes from trying to rely on yourself. However, you are not perfect. You fail, and you live in a fallen world. God wants you to rely on HIM. He wants you to trust that He has the power to help and guide you, and that He WANTS and WILL help and guide you. He does not want you to do life on your own. Trusting Him is believing that He loves you. He wants you to pray to Him about everything in your life.

> **"I am the vine; you are the branches. If you remain in me and I in you, you will bear much fruit; apart from me you can do nothing."**
> John 15:5

To fully trust in God you have to put your confidence in Him, and not in yourself. The good news is that you do not have to do anything to earn God, or go through someone else to find God. You have Him in your heart and He is with you at all times.

> **"And we know that in all things God works for the good of those who love him, who have been called according to his purpose."**
> Romans 8:28

He also has given you His Word to guide you and give you wisdom. The more you develop the discipline of studying God's Word, the more you will be able to hear His directions and His voice. This goes back to the previous month about having your personal quiet time with the Lord. You must transform your mind, and be renewed through God's Word each and every day.

> **"Do not conform to the pattern of this world, but be transformed by the renewing of your mind. Then you will be able to test and approve what God's will is—his good, pleasing and perfect will."**
> Romans 12:2

How has your personal quiet time been going?

_____
_____
_____
_____
_____

If you have been spending time in the Word, do you feel like your confidence, attitudes, and worries have changed? Do you see yourself more hopeful, and more in communication with God? Explain.

_____
_____
_____
_____
_____

Prayer

Read the following scriptures and mediate on them for a while. Take some time to pray to God, thanking Him for loving you and guiding you each step of the way. Pray intentionally, asking God to help you put your trust 100% in Him. Write your prayer below.

> **"Take delight in the Lord, and he will give you the desires of your heart. Commit your way to the Lord; trusting him and he will do this: he will make your righteous reward shine like the dawn, your vindication like the noonday sun."**
> Psalm 37:4-6

> **"Therefore I tell you, do not worry about your life, what you will eat or drink; or about your body, what you will wear. Is not life more than food, and the body more than clothes?"**
> Matthew 6:25

> **"You will keep in perfect peace those whose minds are steadfast because they trust in you."**
> Isaiah 26:3

_____

_____

_____

_____

_____

_____

_____

_____

Activity

Pick one of the scriptures from this week's section and create a poster of it. Write it out bold on paper and even decorate it. Hang it somewhere where you will see it regularly so that you are reminded to trust God. Every time you see it, say a prayer to God giving Him full control because you trust Him.

Week Four
Put It into Practice

Depending on where you are in hearing from God and planning your future, decide what the next step is towards accomplishing these goals. Here is a list of examples for the next step.

- Visit a university or trade school
- Talk with your parents
- Look into going to Bible school
- Talk with your mentor
- Talk to someone who is currently doing what you want to do

Conclusion

Congratulations on a job well done! You have finished Beautiful You and we pray that you have grown in your relationship with the Lord during the process.

As you go forward now as a Christ follower, we have a few words of instruction and encouragement just for you.

1. Make time every day to read your Bible and pray to the Lord. This is how you talk to God and how He talks to you.
2. Find a church and regularly attend it. Get involved in your church. Find the best place for you to serve and discover the joy of giving to others.
3. Develop friendships within the body of Christ. Make sure you surround yourself with other Christ followers who will love, support and inspire you.
4. Pray for your unsaved friends and family. Share the good news of the gospel as the Lord leads you.
5. Know that the Lord loves you and will always walk beside you. His plans for your life are good. As you look to the future, pray for His guidance and direction, and allow your heart to dream big for God and His Kingdom!

www.ingramcontent.com/pod-product-compliance
Lightning Source LLC
Chambersburg PA
CBHW061331040426
42444CB00011B/2858